BIOGRAPHIES

SALLY RIDE
ASTRONAUT, SCIENTIST, TEACHER

Written by Pamela Hill Nettleton
Illustrated by Becky Shipe

Special thanks to our advisers for their expertise:

Philip Chien, Aerospace Writer, Kennedy Space Center, Florida

Susan Kesselring, M.A., Literacy Educator
Rosemount–Apple Valley–Eagan (Minnesota) School District

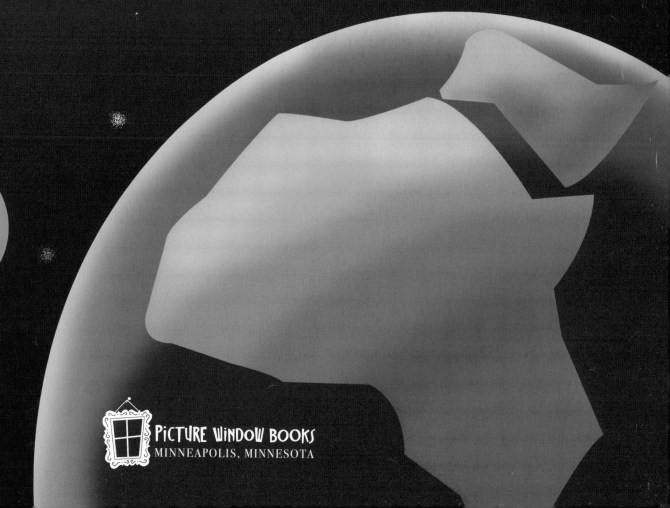

PICTURE WINDOW BOOKS
MINNEAPOLIS, MINNESOTA

Thank you to Philip Chien for his consultation on this book. Philip is an aerospace writer with Earth News, based at the Kennedy Space Center in Florida. He has covered the shuttle program since 1983. The first launch he covered in person was Sally Ride's first spaceflight.

Managing Editor: Bob Temple
Creative Director: Terri Foley
Editor: Peggy Henrikson
Editorial Adviser: Andrea Cascardi
Copy Editor: Laurie Kahn
Page production: The Design Lab
The illustrations in this book were rendered digitally.

PICTURE WINDOW BOOKS
5115 Excelsior Boulevard
Suite 232
Minneapolis, MN 55416
1-877-845-8392
www.picturewindowbooks.com

Printed in the United States of America.

Library of Congress Cataloging-in-Publication Data
Nettleton, Pamela Hill.
Sally Ride : astronaut, scientist, teacher / written by Pamela Hill Nettleton ; illustrated by Becky Shipe.
p. cm. — (Biographies)
Summary: A brief biography that highlights some important events in the life of the first American woman in space.
Includes bibliographical references and index.
ISBN 1-4048-0189-8
1. Ride, Sally—Juvenile literature. 2. Women astronauts—United States—Biography—Juvenile literature.
3. Astronauts—United States—Biography—Juvenile literature. [1. Ride, Sally. 2. Astronauts. 3. Women—Biography.] I. Shipe, Becky, 1977– ill. II. Title.
TL789.85.R53 N48   2004
629.45′0092—dc21   2003004032

In 1983, many Americans were excited for astronaut Sally Ride. Men had traveled to outer space, but Sally was the first American woman to become an astronaut. "Ride, Sally Ride!" the people cheered. Sally's trip in the space shuttle *Challenger* was a big success.

This is the story of astronaut Sally Ride.

The first American woman to blast into space didn't start out wanting to be an astronaut. As a child, Sally Kirsten Ride wanted to play shortstop for the L.A. Dodgers. As a teenager, she wanted a tennis career. Then, she discovered a new dream—and that dream came true.

Sally was born in 1951 and grew up in Encino, California. Her father was a college teacher. Her mother helped women in trouble. Sally's sister, Karen, became a minister. Their parents told the girls to follow their dreams.

Sally was athletic and liked to play football and baseball. She became very good at tennis and got to be on the tennis team at Westlake School for Girls. Later, Sally almost did make tennis her career. But she decided to continue her education instead.

A teacher at Westlake helped Sally see that science was fun. Sally liked her math and science classes. She was a good student and got straight A's in school.

In college, Sally studied physics, the science of natural forces. Later, Sally studied astrophysics, or space science, and she loved it.

After graduate school, Sally found out that NASA, the government space program, was looking for astronauts! She decided to apply.

NASA is short for National
Aeronautics and Space
Administration. Aeronautics
is the science of flight.

NASA

More than 8,000 people wanted to be astronauts. NASA chose only 35. Six of the people were women, and Sally was one of them.

Much hard work lay ahead. First, Sally had to take lots of tests. Some were written tests. Some were athletic contests, like running and swimming.

Sally learned how to fly in high-speed jets and how to parachute. She learned how to scuba dive and survive in the water.

She also learned more about gravity. Gravity is the force that holds things down on the earth. Out in space, gravity works differently. Everything in a spacecraft floats. Sally learned how to eat, drink, and do scientific experiments while floating!

Sally worked hard. It took five years to get ready. In 1983, the day came for Sally and four other astronauts to ride the space shuttle *Challenger.*

Sally was excited! Millions of people would be watching. She was the first American woman and also the youngest American to fly in space. She was only 32 years old and had already done so much. People were proud of her.

Sally was on TV and radio shows. She was in magazines and newspapers. She seemed to be everywhere! People called all this interest in her Sallymania. *Mania* means craziness.

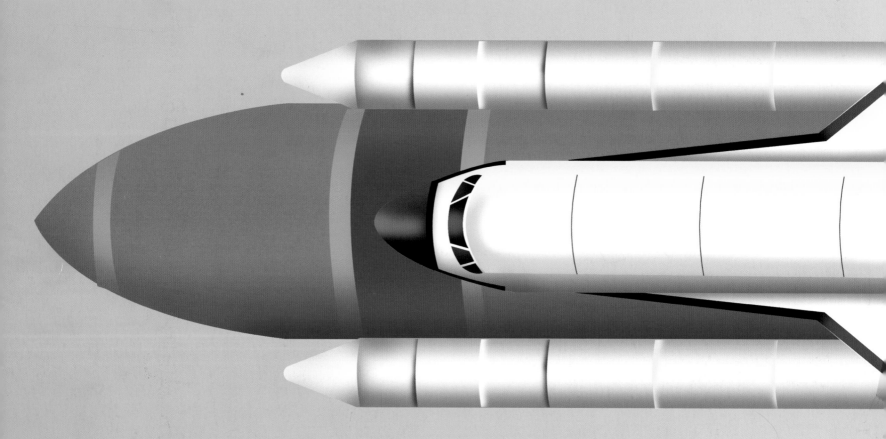

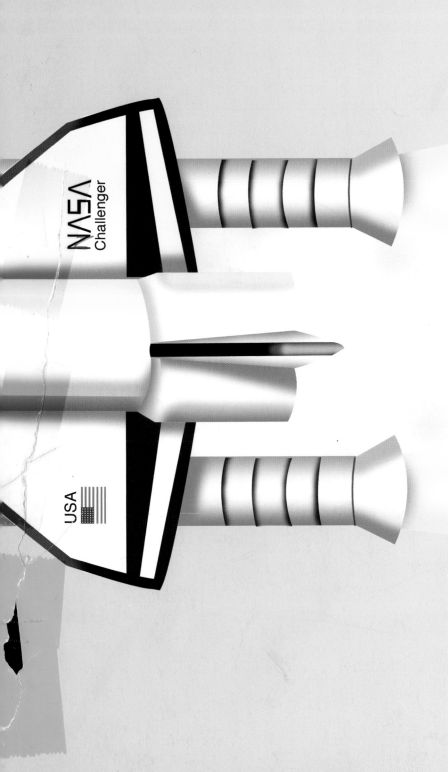

Finally, the day came. An elevator lifted the astronauts high into the air so they could climb through the space shuttle door. They put on their helmets and strapped themselves into their seats. The countdown began.

At blastoff, the shuttle rose with a huge roar and a mass of smoke and flame. It shot into space and flew around Earth for six days.

United States

NASA
Challenger

Sally was a mission specialist.
Mission specialists are responsible
for everything aboard the shuttle
that's necessary for the astronauts
to complete their missions.

The astronauts had work to do. Sally did scientific experiments and helped use a robot arm to release a satellite into space. That satellite took the first photos of a shuttle in orbit.

The crew of the *Challenger* did a good job. The other crew members liked how calm and smart Sally was. When she got back, Sally said she was sure the flight was the most fun she would ever have in her life.

Sally was an astronaut at NASA for eight years.
She flew in space one more time, in 1984.
Then, in 1986, the *Challenger* exploded after liftoff
with another crew aboard. Everyone was shocked
and very sad. Sally was asked to help figure out
what went wrong and make the space program better.

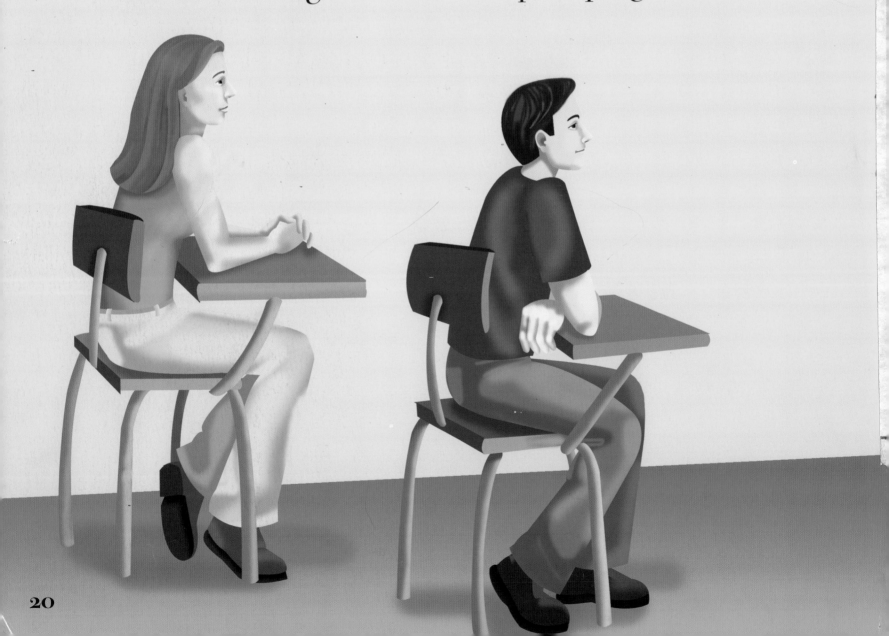

In 1989, Sally Ride became
a teacher of physics at the
University of California.
She especially encourages
girls to study math
and science.

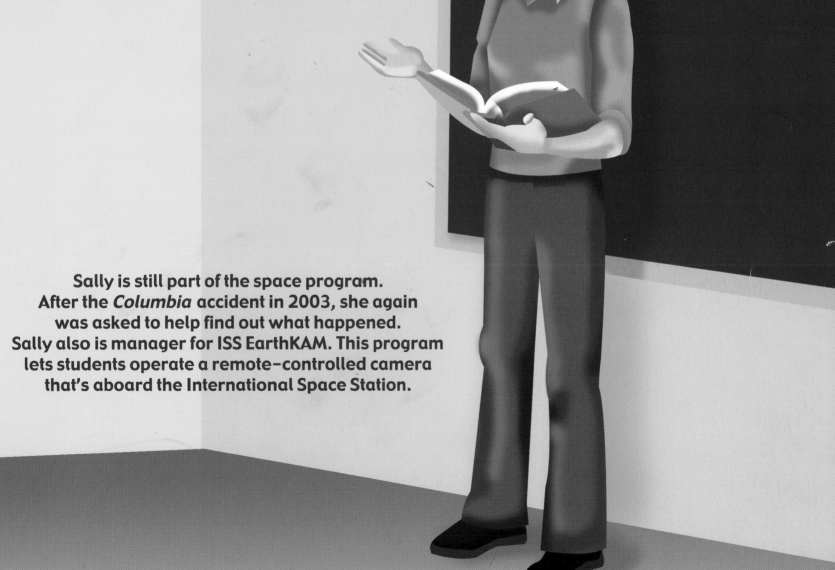

Sally is still part of the space program.
After the *Columbia* accident in 2003, she again
was asked to help find out what happened.
Sally also is manager for ISS EarthKAM. This program
lets students operate a remote-controlled camera
that's aboard the International Space Station.

The Life of Sally Ride

1951   Born in California on May 26

1973   Graduated from Stanford University in California

1978   Joined NASA

1979–87   Was an astronaut at NASA

1983   At age 32, became the first American woman in space
on the seventh *Challenger* space shuttle mission

1984   Took her second space shuttle flight

1989   Became a professor of physics and director of the California
Space Institute at the University of California in San Diego

DID YOU KNOW?

- In June of 2003, Sally Ride was made a member of the Astronaut Hall of Fame.

- Two Russian women went into space before Sally, but Sally was the first American woman. More than 30 American women—as well as women from Canada, Japan, and France—have flown in space.

- You may have experienced low gravity yourself in an elevator going down fast or on a roller coaster after it goes over the top of a hill. The brief, floating feeling you get is actually the effect of reduced gravity. That's because you are falling at the same speed as the elevator or roller coaster. If the elevator or roller coaster went much faster, you would actually float.

- President Ronald Reagan sent jelly beans with Sally and her crew on Sally's first flight. The jelly beans floated around inside the shuttle—until the astronauts caught and ate them all!

- Astronauts don't use drinking glasses. In space, liquid stays in a glass, even if the glass is turned upside down! Astronauts use straws to suck drinks out of containers.

- Sally spent three years learning how to operate the shuttle's huge remote-controlled robot arm to release satellites. Satellites have different jobs. Some help us learn about the weather or the stars. Others carry television signals from place to place.

GLOSSARY

astronaut (ASS-truh-nawt)—someone who travels in space

astrophysics (ass-troh-FIZ-iks)—a science that has to do with objects in space and how they act with one another

experiment (ek-SPER-uh-ment)—a scientific test to see how something works or to try out something

gravity (GRAV-uh-tee)—the force that pulls things toward the earth. Gravity works differently in space.

mission specialist (MISH-uhn SPESH-uh-list)— a scientist or engineer astronaut. Mission specialists are responsible for everything aboard the shuttle that's necessary for the astronauts to complete their missions, or special tasks.

physics (FIZ-iks)—a science that deals with gravity, energy, light, sound, electricity, and other physical forces

remote control (ri-MOHT kuhn-TROHL)—a way to control machines from a distance

satellite (SAT-uh-lite)—a spacecraft that circles around Earth or another heavenly body

space shuttle (SPAYSS SHUHT-uhl)—a spaceship that's made to carry people into space and back

To Learn More

At the Library

Branley, Franklyn Mansfield. *Floating in Space.*
New York: HarperCollins Publishers, 1998.

Jones, Stanley P., and L. Octavia Tripp. *African-American
Astronauts.* Mankato, Minn.: Capstone High/Low
Books, 1998.

Ride, Sally, with Susan Okie. *To Space & Back.* New York:
Lothrop, Lee & Shepard Books, 1986.

Ride, Sally, and Tam O'Shaughnessy. *Voyager: An
Adventure to the Edge of the Solar System.* New York:
Crown Publishers, 1992.

On the Web

FactHound offers a safe, fun way to find Web sites related
to this book. All of the sites on FactHound have been
researched by our staff.
www.facthound.com

1. Visit the FactHound home page.
2. Enter a search word related to this book, or type in this
   special code: 1404801898.
3. Click the FETCH IT button.

Your trusty FactHound will fetch the best Web sites
for you!

On a Trip

See where Sally Ride launched into space
and maybe even watch a launch, too!
Kennedy Space Center Visitor Complex
Kennedy Space Center, FL 32819
(321) 449-4444
Launch viewing information:
(800) KSC-INFO (572-4636)

Index